WILLIAM GRAHAM

Leave The Door Open

WILLIAM GRAHAM

LEAVE
THE DOOR OPEN
BY
WILLIAM GRAHAM

LEAVE THE DOOR OPEN

LEAVE THE DOOR OPEN
WILLIAM GRAHAM

Published By Parables
January, 2019

All Rights Reserved. No part of this book may be reproduced or utilized in any form or by any means, electronic or mechanical, including photocopying, recording, or by any information storage and retrieval system, without permission in writing from the author.

ISBN 978-1-945698-88-0
Printed in the United States of America

Readers should be aware that Internet Web sites offered as citations and/or sources for further information may have been changed or disappeared between the time this was written and the time it is read.

WILLIAM GRAHAM

LEAVE THE DOOR OPEN
BY
WILLIAM GRAHAM

Leave The Door Open

William Graham

Chapter One: Door bell	15
Chapter Two: What Is your Door Made Of?	23
Chapter Three: Door man	29
Chapter Four: Door mat	37
Chapter Five: Door steps	43
Chapter Six: Doors Are Made To	49
Author's notes - Keep Walking	58

Leave The Door Open

The Hidden
OPPORTUNITY

As we find ourselves entertaining a whole new world, it's only right we embrace the secrets hidden within us all.

The kind of secret, once discovered, can change your life. Everyone speaks of change - like it's some wild-haired ritual which entails body swapping or something. When the truth is most of us are scared of opportunity.

I don't know why? But it's true.

Could it be (opportunity brings about change, and change demands we be better than we were yesterday?) That's how I see it. And this comes from a guy who has changed beyond evolution.

How do you define everything you've ever loved and learned being a lie. As if your life is one big episode of a young man who battles struggle to the very end. How do you strive for change when you are serving a 72 year sentence in a Colorado State

Penitentiary? How do you overcome the pressures of gang ties?

How do you inspire others when you haven't been free since 2003? Leaving behind two kids who you've never touched outside of prison walls. Born to a drug abusing mother, who found herself removed from your life because she had to serve a 20 year sentence in 1984 (the same year I was born), born in North Carolina. He has written over thirty four books while incarcerated. He has earned twenty seven certificates of programs involving cognitive thinking. On his off day's he volunteers as a Peer Mentor for a Warden based program which orientates all the new arrival Colorado Department of Corrections offenders. Despite his set backs, Mr. Graham strives to a better person and impact the world.

Acknowledgements

"Everyone I mention here, is guilty of being a real person, who helped me change" -Thank you all.

Ronald "Tiger" Frye, and Marilyn Boykin Frye-I love you both without purpose. R.I.P (karkas •Graham) my baby brother who told me to show the world our struggle.

Tecarra "Ceasar Lawn" Graham, my older brother, who I followed every where.

Evertt M. Harrington, my brother and conrade, who I struggle with and love dearly. I got you.

The Entire Harrington Family, who stood by me during hard times. Thank you.

A warm thank you to Patricia Riley, kyle, and Janisa Guerra-who showed me how good people and family means something to the true ones. Also special thanks to Micheal and Deanna Scadden, who remind me of two turtle doves. Fly high.

Special thanks to Damon "The Nomad" Davis- a guy who deserves the world, and a few bright stars. He is an author, a father, a mentor, and a true brother of the struggle. Thank you.
Thank you to Alex Manigo, who lived a life of scales, up sometimes and down at times, but it all evens out

Special thank you to Chris "C-Mac" Miller, who helped me build an empire from the ground up. Stain Gang forever. Cory Woodard "Lii C"- you are someone who I can say stands on) the ten toes we were designed to stand on. I'm always with you.

Sean Marshall- my brother who gave me insight and divine truth.

A warm hug and beloved embrace for Marquita Rucker, who I call the warrior woman. Her heart is one of a kind. She told me to be the person I was created to be. T T & F

Special thanks to all the kids in my life who I wanted to do better for and inspire. Jaiiyah, Cyprese, Lovely, Essence, Baby Bro, Lii Shugg, and all the kids who are lost in the system.

Special thanks to the staff at D.R.D.C (you guys are very rare and I'll never forget that.

Special thanks to the nursing staff at D.R.D.C and all the ones who showed me the way.

Special thanks to Rory "Big 40" Atkins, who gave me alot of game and stood beside my goals.

Also thanks to Big Les Dawg for being real.

Thank you to Christoher Taylor "CT" who rode with the dream, and showed me true friendship.

Leave the Door Open

Like many young men, William S. Graham struggled to grow up, and search for a higher purpose in life. He found himself stumbling down a dead end road which lead to a disappointing feat.

Then after 15 years in prison, he said enough was enough- as he rediscovered his true direction in life. (empowering others through spoken word and ink dreams)

Putting crime behind him, and focusing on expanding his divine talents.

As a life coach, author, father, mentor, and significant other he is looking forward to the future.

In this impactful book, Graham gives it to you raw and uncut. Giving you the well-needed advice, which shows you how to be powerful and real with yourself.

This book approaches how to overcome the odds of status, statistics, and challenging circumstances.

With motivating wisdom toward goal-oriented support, you will be reminded how special it is to have a break through.

LEAVE THE DOOR OPEN

Graham believes by holding ourselves accountable for our daily limitations, we are granted an over all view of the life we're intended to have.

Chapter One

"Door bell"

Do you hear that ringing sound? The one that you've been pretty much dodging all your life. Yeah, we call that opportunity trying to get in to meet you.

So my question is how long has opportunity been knocking at your door?

I'm guessing since the stone ages.

Don't worry though, we're on a journey toward the best walking you've ever seen. And I'll be your captain on this epic voyage of truth and divine purpose. You can call me Captain Graham. Seriously, don't call me captain Graham!

I'm just a real guy, who has problems like everyone else.

I told myself I would write a book about keeping options open, and here is it.

ACHIEVEMENT

Here's the thing about achievement, it's something you have to constantly chase. You can't wake up with a half-ass effort toward your goals. I mean you can, but you're not going to get the best results you were seeking. You'll get out of it what you put into it (right).

The most important element surrounding the word achievement is effort. Which means you have to put forth the efforts required in order to get the best solution.

And you have to develop a pattern of finishing the things you long to accomplish. It's not an achievement if you don't finish. No matter how small or big the task may be, you have to finish it.

ACCURACY

I recall a time when I started washing cars as a side job. I could wash a car in under 15 minutes.

Foourteen years old, with a pocket full of money - that was me.

But with everything comes a divine lesson to be taught.

I started getting sloppy with each car I washed. (I didn't mean too, it was just so easy to me)

Which brought upon my car washing demise. My boss was informed of my negligence and decided it would be best if

I did not work for him any more. It hurt my heart to hear those words coming out of his mouth. Plus I had built a solid report with my co-workers. We were like a little family of car washers.

But as I said, there's a lesson in everything. I learned that accuracy is very important, not only in business, but in life. right. do it at all.

If you want to do something, you have to do it.

If you don't desire to do it right, then why.

My grandma use to say " if you're going to kill the chicken, the least you could do is cook it!"[11]

What she was expressing to me was the ability to execute when given a task to accomplish. (That chicken didn't even see it coming).

The other lesson I acquired from that scenario gave me a degree to the tenth power. The power of diligence.

I opened up my own cash washing service at a local store a few blocks down from my old job. (Now I was competition)

I cared for every single car I washed, and I took my time washing them.

[11] Never compromise your standards in the face of comfort"

THE BITTER ONES

In life we are asked not to be bitter about the outcome of certain things. We are asked to take the raw sewage of the world, and transform it into gold bars. (Impossible) Especially when these certain things become personal.

Like the job you wanted, but someone else got the position. Does that cause us to be bitter? Yeah, hell yeah!

We are human right!

No one wants to feel over-looked, or discounted. That sucks. But here's a degree to be considered. Have you ever heard of the mountain theory?

It's a theory which states, if you make yourself out to be an ant pile-no matter how productive you may be- people will still step on you or over you. In the same theory, if you make yourself out to be a mountain- people will have to respect you as we respect mountains. There's no one stepping on or over mountains. (Believe that!)

So the only question remains, are you an ant pile or a mountain?

JUST LOOK

You know how when you're driving down the road, not paying attention to any of the signs. Yield. Slow down. Low shoulder. Stop. (Things like that)

That's what it's like when we ignore the signs of chance.

-A total wreck, waiting to happen-

Oddly, I find it quite amusing, how I've never been in a car accident. In my defense, I haven't been in a car in 15 years, unless you're counting prison buses.

In 2006, I sat in a cold prison cell, searching for any form of warmth I could find. (There was none)

My heart and eyes stood emotionless-possibilities

I couldn't find peace any where.

Then I discovered the old paper and pen again. It pretty much embraced me again. But this time something had changed,

I was brighter than I use to be in school. I wanted to help

others with my words. I wanted to relate to the broken hearted. To inspire the hopeless. To ignite the greatest in everyone.

I was a dreamer back then, and between you and I, nothing has changed. Just look within yourself, something is always there.

Possibility

If I asked you to come with me to Las Vegas tonight, would you turn me down? I hope not.

When we get there what games would you play? Would you hit the crap tables? Would you play the slot machines?

Or maybe you want to play bingo huh!

I like rolling dice personally. Dice fascinate me.

A few years back I explored why I like dice so much, and what I discovered left me with an open door perspective.

As we all know, dice are a symbol of chance/possibility.

No matter who you are or where you're from, everyone feels they deserve one chance right!

So say we're in Las Vegas for the night, and I come find you like "hey! I need you to roll these dice for me because I hurt my hand."

LEAVE THE DOOR OPEN

Let's say the table is loaded with money on the line. All you have to roll is a 6, a 9, or a 3, and we can win 50,000 thousand dollars. Imagine how you would feel?

Your heart pounding like a million drums.

What if I told you "if you hit the points, we're going to split the money down the middle."

Does that add a little pressure? What if you really need the money? I bet that changes the perspective. You throw the dice...

they bounce around the table and land.

A solid ten, you were so close we could taste it.

That hurts right! I feel you, but understand when I tell you we didn't quite lose like you think we did.

What we gained from this is the ability to put it all on the line and expose ourselves to chance.

I remember a handful of people who took the gamble of leaving their motherland, only to explore a world they knew nothing about. These same people won with their roll of the dice, and it paid off in a major way.

We now call them pioneers or early settlers who built this country. They weren't perfect, obviously, but what you see is their capability to dance with fate and win.

When we leave the door open, we pr sent ourselves to the world which is attainable.

Our potential isn't limited when we do not close the door for anything that might help us further ongoing prospects.

"You're not a loser when you take a chance, you're a loser when you tell yourself you don't deserve one"

SILENCE

I can't tell you how many alarm clocks I use to walk by back in the day. It was like I suffered from being deaf, when that's not the case.

But for some odd reason we tune out the things we need to hear, and listen to all the nonsense.

Why do we do that?

CHALLENGE

As we begin this new profound path, it gives us great delight in knowing bright things are in our future.

But we have to pay attention to the door bell when it rings.

It could be the one things we've always desired to have.

Leave The Door Open

Chapter Two

What Is Your Door Made Of?

Since the beginning of time people have been walking through door ways to enter places. Some of these places were shabby and others were grand palaces. But one thing they had in common (was the door).

Doors are something we take for granted in our everyday lives. We walk through them, and knock on them- waiting for a sign to enter.

Imagine walking through a door which takes you to the future. re would you go?

Mo t people would desire to go back in time, but who would go forward? A good friend of mine by the name of Chris Miller said he would go forward in time, with high hopes of starting over.

As we enter this chapter ask yourself what am I made of? Yesterday you didn't know this, but today is your awakening ceremony.

Let's get it!

SELF-ESTEEM

Quick question: how do you feel about yourself?

Do you consider yourself to be intelligent? Are you self- sufficient? Do you see yourself as dumb or stupid?

Do you put other people's talents/abilities over yours? It's no secret most people suffer from low self-esteem.

In my opinion, I say people create low self-esteem in themselves. I can see the critics now, prepared to stone me to death if I don't make a solid point in saying that.

Here's the thing, when you look at how people interpret self- esteem, ask yourself why is it so easily misconceived

I believe the pressure from people who suffer self-esteem issues paints an evident picture to the ones who don't. People who suffer from low self-esteem are always asking peoplewithhighself-esteem"whyareyoualwayshappy?"

Or they say "I don't like her because she thinks she's all that!"

Let's get real here, you feel less of a person when those type of people come around you.

Why? you feel attractive? Do you feel talented?

Were you the kind of person who sits home watching TMZ, only hoping to see one of the stars you envy having problems?

I bet it makes you feel good watching Tom Brady lose doesn't it? You're a hater!

But just to let you know you made them perfect in your mind. You and all the magazines, who tell us what is pretty.

What is perfect?

PURPOSE

It's amazing how when I tell people being author wasn't my first dream, they don't believe me.

It's the truth. Up until 2006 I hadn't wrote anything, yet alone books. My first love was producing music, and I never wrote my lyrics down on paper. (Great memory)

When I did discover the paper and pen, it was like a fish to water. I enjoyed it. It felt like a super power or some secret identity that no one knew about.

But there was only one problem with my new profound

I felt like a man who is late for an important meeting, but can't find his way through the darkness to get to it.

That was a very frustrating time for me, but I kept writing. Out of the fire produced a worthy diamond to display, as I found my purpose in art.

Self-help books gave me a sense of relation and fulsome that even I didn't see coming. I was at peace for the first time in my life.

Just as I found my purpose in life, I whole heartedly believe everyone has a gift buried deep inside their soul.

It's just waiting to come alive inside you.

ACCEPTANCE

You must first accept yourself before demanding others to seek worthiness in you-

There's an unspoken state of mind that goes with being accepted by others. We all long to fit in with the cool kids - they seem to party better than the rest of us.

But part of leaving your door open is empowered by

recognizing how unique you are in your own right.

Which means you don't have to fit in when you can create your own lane. By making it your own, you make people desire to be around you.

Call it crazy but humans are attracted to things that we can't have or things that pay us no attention. Which works the same way if you make yourself the "it" factor by not running to be accept by others. Just let it happen, it'll come to you.

"'Live your life as if what you should be doing doesn't exist"

POWER

Just like many males who came before me, power has a way of drawing a very vivid picture.

I remember during my football years in high school, I learned a valuable lesson about power.

There was this rival team who we couldn't defeat to save our lives. Throughout our school histories, we had lost many great battles to them. And this one year showed zero signs of change on the horizon. I even recall our football coach,

Mr. Anderson, putting the whole team on a bus to attend one of their games. So imagine sitting in the bleachers watching them slaughter another team.

Forty-two points compared to the other team who had ten points was the final score. I couldn't help but ask Coach Anderson why he is smiling through the whole game?

He calmly said " every titan has a weakness."

I didn't quite understand what he was saying at the time, but knowing him- I knew something was formulating in his mind.

The next week or so our practices were a little different and slightly bizarre. Coach Anderson made a few local calls, which resulted in our entire starting line playing a real college football team.

Their level of fitness was impeccable to say the least. I didn't even see them drinking water.

They were androids with nice compliments. Meaning every time we tried to tackle them they would pat us on the back and say "good try little man!"

They beat us so bad they stopped keeping score, if I had to put a score on it, I would say eighty nine points to twenty-one points.

I believe some of our football players went to the hospital.

But the lesson was every titan has a weakness, and Coach Anderson challenged us to find one in our rival team. After watching multiple film from their team, we were able to pin point their weakness.

(They exhausted themselves after the first half of each game.)

And we were a second half type of team already, so it was lunch time for us.

I don't want to brag or nothing, but we beat them like they stole something. They were crying after the game and hugging each other like someone died or something.

We patted them on the back and calmly said "good try little man!"

"Power is the ability to control a situation and use energy to get work done"

LOVE IS BIGGER

There's a word we all long to say, but find it resting on the tip of our tongues. That word is "Love."

A word which demands maturity from all.

I remember being young in love, and confused as a dog in a rabbit costume. (Notice I said dog)

That would be one of the words my past girlfriends would use to describe me back then.

I was very childish when it came to the relationship department. I didn't know what I wanted, so like a kid at a buffet, I wanted it all.

But eventually I grew up, and begin understanding how love isn't to be played with, or tossed around.

Here is a passage someone once told me about love.

"Love is bigger than your ego. You might say it is not, but ask yourself which one has survived broken homes, and being alone? Your ego or love? Which one is Googled a billion times a day? Which one can't you buy or sell?

Which one is universal?

Which one can you live with forever?"

Growing up is a part of life, and love is part of that life.

Chapter Three

"Door man"

When you hear the word "door man", what comes to mind?

A person on duty at the door to a large building. Someone who has the power to grant you or deny you access to a building.

It's quite amusing how some door men are polite and others are donkey faces. But in the last 20 years, due to all the tragic bombings, doormen have earned a little more respect- wouldn't you agree?

Alright, now we're getting somewhere!

Let's say your body is a magnificent building with grand opport- unity inside.

And as you see, every organ in your body-building serves a utilizing position.

Now let's make your mind the doorman of this body-building of yours. In which you must ask yourself, what kind of doorman am I? Are you stern and protective, suspicious of every little thing? Do you fall asleep on the job, unaware of the grand opportunities and certain dangers?

Or are you the type of doorman who never shows up for work?

In this chapter, we'll explore most of the things that hold us back from succeeding in life. And we'll also address your doorman abilities and disabilities.

THE BURGLARY

Imagine if you came home to discover your residence has been burglarized. You look around, only to find the things you hold dear to your heart are gone.

Your lap top with all your multiple documents on it, gone. The jewelry your grandmother brought you, when you were a child, gone. Your rent money, gone.

Everything-gone.

Imagine if after three weeks, the authorities inform you they've found the person who raided your home. They show you a picture of them. It's you in the picture.

Most of us rob ourselves every day, not taking materialistic things, b ut we vandalize our dreams and opportunities.

We steal these things from ourselves, and wonder if our Fed X packages h a v e been stolen. (That's called limited vision)

When we do not see the obvious things in our lives, but desire to see change, it's like searching for sand in a desert.

PEOPLE PROBLEMS

Do you have people problems? Do some people just make your skin crawl when they come around you? When these people you don't like are talking, do you roll your eyes, or want to jump up and drop kick them in the teeth?

Congratulations! You have people problems.

Don't freak out, it's not a big deal. Everyone dislikes someone.

But here's the alcohol in your eggnog, ask yourself what is it about that one particular person you don't like?

You have to get down to the root of the problem, only then will you be able to get pass it. Who knows, it might even help you to be a better person.

Like for instant, I had this very beautiful young lady one time, which was a long time ago- don't judge me- but anyway, she was beautiful but a compulsive complainer. Every where we went she hated, or found something wrong with the place.

We would go out to the movies, and the movie was too loud. We would go to a football game, and a bug flew in her mouth. (Thank you bug)

No matter what happened in her life, she would complain abundant- ly. One day I told her I couldn't do it anymore. I had to get away from her. She was negative energy.

Sometimes our people problems keep us from walking through the doors of potential. (That's not healthy)

We Need To Talk

If you could put three versions of yourself in a room to have a conversation how would it go?

But if we are going to do this we might as well make it a little interesting.

Let's say the three versions of yourself are 10 years apart.

One is 20 years old, one is 30 years old and the other one is 40 years old.

We ask them questions to pick their brains. The first question is for the 20 year old "you". What do you want out of life?

The second question is for the 40 year old "you".

If you could give these other two some advice, do you think they would listen?

The last question is for the 30 year old "you".

What the hell is wrong with you?

Sorry about that last question, I just figured your 30 year old version of you was like the 30 year old version of me (afew years back) totally confused.

Now imagine what would be said if they could speak to each other.

How would you handle the 20 year version of you talking disrespectful to the 30 year version of you?

Would you want to fight him or should I say yourself?

Would the 40 year version of you desire to settle the whole thing in a peaceful manner? Just remember the importance of self is something reflected not only in the present, but also in the future to come.

A THRONE

I remember learning a particular lesson growing up, which resonates with me even until this day.

My uncle was a grade A certified loser to the 9th power.

The whole family knew it. He was constantly harrowing money from whoever he could con or make feel sorry for his situation. He found himself sleeping on so many people's couches, the lining in his back was completely wrecked.

I can't recall a time when he didn't smell like some kind of alcoholic beverage. A true lush at heart.

Anyway, my grandmother told me on numerous occasions, "you can be anything you want to be, just don't be like him!"

This was one of her own sons she was talking about,

After couch surfing on grandma's couch for many years, he left a permanent imprint where he would sleep. Well it wasn't long before even grandma had enough of his total neglect for her things. One day while cleaning the house, she demanded I throw out the alcohol reeking couch my uncle slept on. I did with joy.

Would you believe my uncle and a few of his bum friends picked the couch up off the curb, and sat it under a tree.

It was like a bum's club house...for drinkers and smokers.

I remember running into the house to tell my grandma about what my eyes had just seen.

She was watching her favorite TV. program when I busted through the door. I said "grandma! Uncle Rob is sitting on the couch we threw out, with his bum friends."

She said the most profound thing I've ever heard. She said "a king to his throne"

The lesson I learned from the wisdom of my grandmother was, in life we are all granted what we feel we are owed.

Some of us find ourselves stumbling through life, trying

to make it up as we go along, but quickly discover how hard it is to fake the truth.

Now as I look back on that situation, it makes me wince knowing the only mother my uncle knew had lost respect for him. And even more depressing knowing he had lost respect for himself.

SIMPLICITY!

If I had a dollar for every time I complicated a simple situate- ton, I'd be the richest man on the face of this earth.

I have been complicating things in my life since I was a young boy. There are so many lessons which can be shared with you guys, and some of them are outlandish.

Like for instance, this one time I wanted to go to this after party, which as you know took place after my curfew.

Everyone in school was talking about it, plus a girl I liked mentioned she would be there. I had to go.

So I plotted on my escape as soon as my aunt left for the night shift she was working. I had to sneak out the window because my little brother was a notorious snitch at the time. Spate!!

Soon as I jumped out of my window I was met by a slush of mud ,which was the results of a rainy day now passed.

I said so many curse words walking down the street,you'd think I was trying to wale up the dead.

It wasn't long before I reached my best friend's house, and used their water hose out back to rinse the mud off my shoes.

A slight smirk on my face indicated the first win of the night was all mine.

The after party was already jumping once we arrived around 12:35 am. Surveying the room, I noticed everyone had a drink in their hands- so I grabbed a cup. As I poured out whatever fruity non-sense they were drinking, I seen a slue of faces waiting to see why? The attention felt good.

See what none of these square kids knew was my partner, Duke and I, had brought to the party was some hard core liquor. Everyone was so quick to ask "what is that?"

We looked at them like they were babies, and quickly shot a humorous remark, "this that grown man stuff right here!" The party went as cool as a fan could spin, I had no com- plaints at all. I even got a chance to walk that special girl home, and cop me a couple of good feels in before she put the brakes on my race car.

(She was worth the wait, so I played it like a handful of aces)

I wish some of that cool would have prepared me for my aunt@sitting in the living room chair once I tried creeping in real slow. When she asked me where I had been, would you know she didn't even care about the time. I got in trouble for having liquor on my breath. (I should have kept it simple)

Just like many of us who find the constant need to make our lives more difficult than they already are, we over think the situation. Putting ourselves in a state of panic and confusion.

Part of leaving the door open has to do with our urges to to reform, and go back to doing what we are comfortable doing. (That's a big No! NO!)

Someone once told me, "you can make your life chess, or you can make your life ping pong...it all depends on how you want to play."

Sometimes I tell myself if something is stopping you from doing something stupid, let them do their job.

FORGIVENESS

As we take a long, hard look at our lives- we must ask our inner selves "why is forgiveness so important?"

Forgiveness leaves a bad taste in everyone I meet mouths, it's like one of the hardest things to do. Why?

Because you and I feel like forgiveness + pain equals "weak". I use to feel the same way, and honestly, there are many prays that save a lot of people. I'm not the first person to forgive the people who hurt me. (Which is strange) seeing how at one point in time, I needed my victims to forgive me.

Realizing that allowed me to actually get off my high horse, only to understand "nobody's perfect."

I left the door open for new thought, when it made me uncomfortable. That's where I found a piece of my growth- hidden under 200lbs of pain. Countless of times we find ourselves keeping secrets from our own hearts, afraid to pull the rug out and sweep it.

Chapter Four

"Door mat"

In this chapter we explore what it means to be stern and reserved on certain matters which effect your life.

We high light how people sometimes attempt to take advantage of an open door policy.

Just because we understand this new profound state of mind, we are no one's door mats.

You can't wipe your feet on us, and we won't sit outside your house patiently until you come and get us. Those days are over-

That's our new model.

NON-CONFORMITY

The world is full of people who refuse to drink the kool-aid, which gets passed around.

If you're reading this, and saying to yourself, "why do I seem so different than everyone else?"

Well, you could be what many people call a non-conformist.

A non-conformist understands the standards of life, but

has a constant need to break away from the day to day.

They usually have their own style, and state of ideas that over throw any kind of standards. They are quick to disagree with your ideologies if they feel your perspective is beyond erroneous. So in short, if you're on some grade A bull sh*t, they are likely to call you on it.

To the general public, non-conformist, seem to be harsh and insensitive. (That's not true)
True non-conformist don't mean to hurt your feelings, they just can't let you push your hokum over their beautiful floor of thoughts.
"The power to be conscious is a gift from the higher accords"

HONESTY

It's no shock, we live in a candy coated world full of sweet bubble wrap. Everyone is so up tight, afraid to speak their minds-like what happened to saying the real and living it? Where did all the real people go? Mars maybe!

I don't quite know, but I do know this- the truth is well-needed in this sweet booty world.

I know everybody can't be that washed up, especially to the point where we don't tell people what's on our mind. Sometimes you have to close a chapter in order to turn the page, and finish the book

So let's say it's someone at work, who you have been waiting to tell them what's really on your mind (now the time) Don't be mean about it, but give it to them hard enough or them to feel it.

DROWNING MAN

I'm sure you may have heard the saying "a drowning man doesn't have many friends". Why?

A drowning man is in a state of panic, and is willing to pull anyone down with him. He'll use you as a floating device to keep his head above water. He's a true coward at heart.

Scared to die, and afraid to live.

I've seen plenty of drowning men in my time, broken and confused.

Most drowning men turn to religion when they feel as if the water is rising, but like a true coward, they drop their grace at the first sight of day light.

Here's one of my favorite stories I like to tell.

There once was a man who got lost in the woods. Everyone who came with him had moved on with their lives. For many years there was no sightings of him. He was just another lost soul among the woods.

Every night he would look up at the stars and pray to God someone would come and rescue him, but for many years no one came. He ate berries and whatever he could find to survive. He made due and he survived.

One day out the blue, a helicopter found him

He was so happy.

After being home for so long, the man begin to miss the woods.

He would often fantasize about leaving everyone behind, only to return to his state of peace.

He would say "in the woods, I didn't have to worry about other people!"

"In the woods no one made me go to work" "I ate what I wanted to eat."

"I did what I wanted to do."

It wasn't long until he returned back to the woods, only to find a construction company had tore the woods down.

All the trees were cut down and nothing was the same as he knew it would be.

Walking back to his home, he said to himself what am I to do now?

He looked up at this sign in his neighborhood which read (Live).

FRIENDSHIP

After watching 15 years of the show "Survivor", I can truly say the word friendship has a shaky ring to my ears.

See just like in the show, you eat someone, and everything seems rosy red. Then out of no where, you get a chance to meet the real them. (The person they hide from the world) Trust me when I tell you I know what it is like to be that guy who feels stupid for putting my trust in another person. But I also can tell you what it feels like to put the knife in someone's back. (Figuratively)

I'm not trying to start anything, but consider this notion.

Say you found 2 million dollars, but had to put it in someone's name- who would you trust to give you back your money?

I can hear all the gullible babies now saying, "I would put it in my mother's name or in my father's name- they would never steal a dime from me!"

In some cases this statement is right on the money, but I can honestly say everyone doesn't know the true definition of friendship.

True friendship is only reflected when comrades have went to battle for what they believe in, and constantly maintain the remembrance.

SEXUALITY
RATIONALITY

We're all adults here, let's address an issue which constantly haunts the work place everyday. "Sexuality" without a shadow of doubt plays a vital role in how we view our co-workers, and our bosses.

Women are being paid less money to perform equal duties of men, which I agree doesn't make sense at all. If you can do the job -you deserve the pay (It'sthat simple).

PASSION

Another issue giving the work place a black eye is the loosestate of passion, that starts off red hot(only)to burnout bitterly. I'm not saying you shouldn't leave the door pen for new love, I'm just pointing out, the board room and the bedroom is different.

......Sometimes it's safe to cool our shorts, and use that big brain which got us the job in the first place.

Remembering broken hearts heal very slow when everyone knows.

Leave The Door Open

Chapter Five

"Doorstep"

When taking the proper steps needed, to get to the door of opportunity, we must remember it's not always rainbows and pixie dust. Like everything in life, we have to be willing to take those steps which elevate us toward the door we've been waiting to walk through.

Before we get started- ask yourself, what prevents me from taking that first step?

FLEXIBILITY

Have you ever heard of the phrase "stick in the mud?"

That would be the best way to describe how my personality use to be. I had no flexibility when it came to certain things.

I'm not proud of it, but I don't regret how I use to see life.

It gave me a lot of divine insights to help me grow pass the things in life, which gave me the most troubles.

Like for example: I wish I had a better sense of handling problems when I was younger. (Sounds odd I know) But not having this new profound gift made me cherish it even more.

I now understand the importance of being able to laugh and let water roll off your back, instead of always having to be on point like a guard dog.

Some of us have to loosen up a little, start enjoying the true nature of life. Once we do that, doors will open for us.

I use to say "no one is going to get over on me- I watched** everyone. I watched everyone but myself.

Sometimes we cheat ourselves of the things we have coming, then wonder why we don't have things.

NOGAMY!

With all due respect, I say , why get married if you don't love someone? Don't you dare say safety and security, because that non-sense is a dying art of getting by. You're afraid! There's nothing wrong with being afraid, but please don't spend multiple years feeling trapped in a fallacy.

Telling yourself you're in a happy relationship, when the truth is you one second away from jumping off a bridge. Monogamy isn't for everyone, I know that now, but at one time I felt quite different than this. I felt everyone should find someone special-giving them a lasting love to always cherish and hold dear. (Sounds good!)

Sometimes our story book ideas are far-fetched and a one size fits all type of regard.

Not saying there's not a special kind of love out in the world just for you. I'm just saying if you truly love that special person of yours, make sure it's real. Don't be with someone just because they have money or power (that sucks).

You have to leave the door open for someone who is waiting to enter your life.

GROWTH

In recent years, we've seen a spike in divorce rates which have become very alarming. I wonder why?

I have a theory but it's just one thing in a giant battle of why people are separating.

My theory takes us back to a day and age when our great grand- parents ruled the land. A time when respect had a place to call home. Back when, if you liked someone, it was no crime to go on as many dates needed to build the bond.

It was almost like they were taking the proper steps to get to a goal, instead of rushing into a situation head first.

My theory is supported by the lack of romance we do in our everyday relationships. No one is taking their time with the entity of dating any more.

At the first sign of affection, we are getting married, only to find how inexperienced we are. Not to add, we give up on the relationship/marriage at the first sign of trouble.

As if we are unaware of certain faults in people, including the ones we love.

When we truly accept others for who they are, or who they are destine to be- its best to get a clear understanding about why we connect with one another.

GENEROSITY

Growing up in the south, I was groomed to see generosity as a way of life. Every house hold on my block knew each other in some form or way. I use to despise the fact my friends and I couldn't get away with anything mischievous, simply because someone in the neighborhood would always give us up. But I also enjoyed the closeness of having a huge family outside my immediate family.

In today's society I feel less of a personal approach toward giving or caring for others. Of course you have your stars and TV. personnel who donate as a way of caring (tax write off) style, but the intentions are real- I hope.

Anyway, I just wanted to share with you guys something that helped me out a lot. The more I gave-the more I got.

I know it sounds quite strange when you look around and don't feel you have anything to give. Sometimes giving your time, or your man power/human power is more than you know. It helps. Any time there is a national' disaster a helping hand is always needed. Sometimes a simple conversation with someone who is struggling is enough to make an impact on the world.

"We are all on this spinning rock together, let's act better than we were before"

BABY BOTTLES

If you were walking down a busy street, and seen a grown man drinking from a baby bottle, what would you think1

Let me guess, you'd probably say he was crazy, or mentally challenged. Or better yet, some kind of freaky fetish type of guy.

Don't worry, I would too. Anyone with good sense would be compelled to think there was something wrong with the guy. We're not being judgmental by thinking these things, its just the way we are wired.

By highlighting the notion of adulthood, we understand

how some things just do not fit.

You know how some things throw you for a loop? Like for an example/ say you were driving down a country back road, arid seen a cow standing on top of a barn. How would your face look? I'm guessing it would look quite shocked to be viewing what you'd be seeing. And if no one was around to see it as well,

I 'm willing to bet you would pull out your phone and record it. Here's- another grenade in your chicken noodle soup. Everything has its own time.

What does that mean?

It means you shouldn't be trying to squeeze your mommy legs into your daughter's jeans every chance you get.

You're not 16 years old anymore. I don't care how many face cream products you have, it still doesn't change the fact that you are aging just like the rest of us.

Sorry to be the bearer of bad news, but someone had to tell you.

There's nothing more hilarious than seeing a 40 year old person inthe club with 20 year old people.

Their like the kid who was suppose to graduate high school 3 years ago, but they are still hanging around.

That's just creepy.

Here's some sound advice, act your age, not your shoe size. RIP Prince.

OMEBACKSTRONGER

I remember my 9th grade year in high school, I tried out for the varsity football team. I wanted it so badly.

My older brother had did great on the same team before leaving for college, which added a level of pressure to go along wigth the nerves to do good.

Most of the coaches knew me on a first name basis, so I didn't want to disappoint their expectations.

Before practice started I was already on the field prepared to do my thing to the tenth power.

First we started with running drills, then did a few work outs to test everyone's level of speed.

I wanted to be the starting wide receiver, which as you know is a very ballsy move for a freshman. (Ididn't care)

I told myself I was the man for the job.

After the try outs I walked away with a grand smile glued to my face.

A few days later a piece of paper was posted in the school hallway with the names who had made the team.

I scanned down the list in search of my name, it wasn't on the list. (I thought to myself, this must be some kind of mistake)

Sadly after talking to football coach I discovered

Football is a religion down south, and when I tell you I could crawl into a ditch and die...it's not a lie.

One day while throwing the football in my own back yard, I was talking to my baby brother about not making the team. Sounding all depressed and stuff. He refused to throw me a pity party. He told me in plain words "don't worry about it bra, just come back stronger next year!"

That's what I did, and everyone knew it.

I shared this piece with you guys because I wanted you to know that sometime you don't make the first cut.

Sometimes the other guy gets the job.

But if you have moxie, trust me when I say to you "come back stronger!"

Chapter Six

"Doors Are Made To Be Opened"

You know how when you're watching a scary movie, on the edge of your seat, wondering what's coming next? Your heart is racing and your eyes are darting back and forth like a crazy person. You can feel the hairs on the back of your neck standing straight up. Then a door opens-bone chilling results.

Most of us treat chance and possibility like afraid to walk through the door of life

(That's crazy when you consider how hypocritical we are)

It's like we play the lottery of life, unprepared for what happens if we win. Unaware that doors are made to be opened.

COOPERATION & CONTRIBUTION

"When people want to help you, let them"

Call it what you may, but no one likes to feel stepped on or left out. Like I always say- it's in our nature to connect o one another. (Corny but true)

I also believe everyone has something to bring to the table of life. Now everything which gets brought to the table isn't a brick of gold, but you know how that goes.

Even myself, I would be lying if I told you all my ideas are worth applauding. Some of my early ideas were quite stupid, and it took time to train my brain sufficiently.

But I didn't close the door on my potential to be better, and get better in time.

Too many times we see people pulling on doors to get them open- afraid to ask for help. Or maybe they're too prideful to admit they can't do something by themselves. (It's alright Batman!)

We understand you have issues asking others for help, I believe we all struggle with that at one point and time of our lives. Once again I am guilty of the same crime (pride). I'm talking about growing up in foster homes and adoption agencies gave me an early bitter taste about people helping me.

"I don't need anyone's pity!" That's what I use to tell people who tried to help me. I couldn't differentiate between the people who wanted to help me, and the ones who pitied me.

I had to learn the difference between the two, and I grew from this state of mind. Now when I help others, I'm very aware of the message I send to others.

NOT IMPORTANT to ME

With all we know about behavior science, is it safe to say we're all crazy. I could go a long with that notion. Matter fact, we're not crazy- we're challenged.

At times we close the door of blessings, which are destine to come our way regardless of what we do. These blessings are due to come our way, but why should we delay them.

It's just like when someone stops by your house, but you're not home, so you miss out on whatever blessing was destine to come your way. Sometimes it's a good thing to miss out on certain blessings, and sometimes it's a bad thing.

The major thing we can take from this is the fact that we shouldn't cut ourselves off from the promptness of our daily blessings.

"If you look mad all the time people will be hesitant to approach you"

Fix your face!

SELF-CONTROL

When I was a young boy, I recall having a very vicious temper which had a habit of coming out during sport activities. I hated to lose. Losing made me feel like I was helpless, and being helpless gave me purpose. A purpose to be better than my dead beat father, or my confused mother.

A purpose that got loss in the broken state of disappointment.

A purpose I had to go searching for after many years of denied talents. Reminding myself it was still out there, and I needed it to be whole again. I didn't quit.

My first step was recognizing who I was? Which is very import- ant in the major goal of discovery.

The second step was learning how to fight the impulse of

my first nature. Which seems like torture at first- a bold type of torture. But after many pitfalls, I found a sense of peace in myself. I found something in my lost. I found strength. The kind of strength which helps you control a temper, like I had.

Positive vs. Negative

If I had a magic wand, my first order of business would be to change all the negative people into positive, productive people. Instantly, they would jump up and start cutting grass, or running a 500 fortune club.

But sadly, I don't have a magic wand with those capabilities. What I do have is the power to effect how you view yourself, and how you view others.

The main thing you need to know is there's two type of people in this world (chairs and ladders).

Chairs are the kind of people who sit down and complain about the things they desire to change.

Ladders are the people who climb to reach new heights, and demand to be better than they were yesterday.

So my question to you is simple, (are you a chair or a ladder?)

Chairs wish they were like ladders

.Up beat attitude

Pays attention to detail

Willing to learn

.Achieves goals

HUMOR

Hands down my favorite comedian is Eddie Murphy. His humor has no bounds if you ask me. Truthfully, Eddie Murphy doesn't even have to say anything to make you laugh, his look alone can bring a tear to your eye. Or what about that crazy ass laugh of his. (The guy is the truth)

The reason why I brought him up was to address a gift that some people have, and others don't. The gift of humor. Humor is like singing everyone sounds good in the shower, but the day job isn't in jeopardy behind it.

Here's the thing about humor, if you don't have it-don't force it. Many people turn their bosses or guest off with stupid, weak jokes that never hit home. (You are no Eddie Murphy!)

The quicker you discover that, the better off we'll all be.

Now don't get me wrong, you can become very skilled at that particular craft, but it takes work. If you're willing to put in the work to attain such a gift, then you will have them bowing down to your feet as well.

And if you got, let it loose like a mad dog off a leash.

SITTING DOWN ON LIFE

Here's a degree I recently discovered, but always knew about. You know how babies are always crawling from one place to be in a timely manner. Where are they going?

Its like they're lead by their own curious instincts to be that way.

Leave The Door Open

Here's the kicker about the whole entity of babies, they refuse to let anything hinder their missions. We have no idea where they are going, but they do.

One day I tested this baby theory of mine. While baby sitting my nephew, I noticed how he started crawling out the living room. At first I would go grab him and bring him back to where I was watching TV.

Again he would attempt a daring escape from the living room, which after a few times frustrated me.

The first thing I realized was no matter how many times I picked him up and brought him back, he would still try to crawl away. The second I realized was this baby is in better shape then me. (Divine Intervention)

Instead of grabbing him and bringing him back to the living room, I simply followed him to where he was headed.

Would you believe my tiny little nephew crawled to the bedroom, where my pit bull puppy was sleeping and laid beside it.

I smiled from ear to ear watching them together. They were like two friends taking a nap beside one another. But here's the part where you ask yourself, how did my nephew know to crawl into my bedroom where my puppy was sleeping?

He didn't hear my puppy making any noise or whimpering, so how did he know to go accompany it in the room?

Instincts maybe!

I believe we all are born with a sense of curiosity, which we have been trained to ignore on a daily basis.

Why?

Because as we get more into tech-world, it shows we fade away from the things built directly into our DNA.

You don't see Spider Man ignoring his spider senses do you? "I got a good feeling about this!"

Remember how people use to say that?

All they're saying is (I'm trusting my instincts on this one) and you trust yours by trusting them.

Trust me when I tell you instincts are all animals have at times.

When an antelope hears something in the brush, it doesn't sit back and analyze the grass. It runs.

It doesn't feel stupid for running, while a human would second guess the dash out of looking foolish. (that's foolish)

So if your instincts tell you to get up off your mother's couch and go back to school, that's exactly what you do.

Don't fight the feeling! Invite the feeling!

A HOME RUN

It is said most baseball players envision themselves hitting a home run. Some even listen to pre-recorded tapes of giant crowds to get the full experience.

Let's look at your life as if you were a major league base ball player. As of lately your batting average has been quite low. You find yourself spending more time in the batting cage, trying to raise that average.

First of all, you must ask yourself (why do I want to win?)

That's a good question.

Many would say, "I want to win because I hate losing!"
Simple enough right!

But let's look a little deeper into why?

Personally, I dislike the feeling of letting people down. If I look at the people I care about as my team mates, why wouldn't I want them to be proud of me?

Why wouldn't I desire to put smiles on their faces?

Understandably, we know every game in life is not to be won, but also refusing to apply ourselves is a grave travesty.

If we apply ourselves to whatever we desire, it is clear that our percentage of attaining it will increase. (It's that simple)

"Some people swing at life, with clear intentions to knock the ball out of the park..do you?"

PERSONAL VALUES

Do you lie to yourself?

Most people do. They get up in the morning, like you and I do, take a shower, make a cup of coffee, and tell themselves a bold face lie.

The lie becomes an excuse, which protects their ideologies on a daily basis.

They tell the selves their happy when they know it's a lie. The truth is they're unhappy about how their careers have stagnated. They're unhappy in their dry-why relationships. They're unhappy about their kids, who don't talk to them, or show them any respect.

But here's the thing, you can't keep lying to yourself about what is really going on in your ife. Hiding your ain from the world, and judging others.

Everyone can see you are not happy. It's written all over your face. So why not leave the door open for someone to come help you?

Why stay closed off from any one who could relieve your pain? Some times just talking to people with a common bond helps the situation.

"Remember the power resides in leaving the door open"

PERSONAL VALUES

.Trust

.Honor

.Love

.Independence

.Loyalty

.Compassion

.Intelligence

.Family

What are your personal value?

AUTHOR'S NOTE

After reading this book I hope you feel I did my sole duty, sharing thoughts and connecting to others.

One thing I know to be true is - if you're unhappy in your life…

, nothing won't work the way you desire it to play out. Just go ask all the celebrities who have everything a human soul could ask for, but some things are *not* sold or given. Like personal values and peace.

William Graham

LEAVE THE DOOR OPEN

WILLIAM GRAHAM

www.ingramcontent.com/pod-product-compliance
Lightning Source LLC
Chambersburg PA
CBHW050207130526
44591CB00035B/2362